Discovering Your Destiny

Other books by the author:

How to Have Victory Over Sin
Effective Evangelism
Intimacy With God

Discovering Your Destiny

How to know God's will for your life

Floyd McClung Jr.

with Geoff and Janet Benge

Marshall Pickering

Marshall Morgan and Scott
Marshall Pickering
3 Beggarwood Lane, Basingstoke, Hants RG23 7LP, UK

First published in 1988 by Marshall Morgan and Scott
    Publications Ltd
Part of the Marshall Pickering Holdings Group
A subsidiary of the Zondervan Corporation

British Library CIP Data

McClung, Floyd
  Discovering your destiny.
  1. Christian life – For young persons
  I. Title
  248.4'024054

ISBN: 0 551 01730 9

Text set in Plantin by Brian Robinson, Buckingham
Printed in Great Britain by Cox and Wyman, Reading

Contents

Acknowledgement

I wish to express my indebtedness and appreciation to Geoff and Janet Benge who helped write this booklet. Their names should really be on the cover.

Geoff and Janet have been faithful friends and wonderful co-authors. Many of the ideas shared here came through the stimulation of conversations with them in meeting places as varied as Bozeman, Montana and Amsterdam, Holland.

Thank you Geoff and Janet, for your friendship and for standing with me through the development of this booklet. I am very grateful.

Floyd McClung
Amsterdam, Holland

What is my Destiny?

My 12 year old daughter, Misha announced that her summer camp leader had told her that every person has a special destiny for their life. 'What is my destiny, Daddy?' she asked as we strolled down one of Amsterdam's beautiful cobblestoned streets. Thus began a long afternoon of discussing the concept of God's destiny for each of our lives, and how we can discover it.

There are times when each of us asks the same question. We all want to know what God has in store for us in the future. We puzzle as to whether it takes years of clever detective work to discover God's will, or if it's plain and easy to find. This question affects whom we will marry, our profession, where we live, and how we respond to unfolding opportunities for ministry.

In a world of so many choices it's not always easy to know in which direction we should be heading as Christians. Opportunities seem to abound. There are many open doors in front of us, and even a few tantalizing closed doors! More than ever we need to know that God is leading us in the decisions we make and the direction we take in life.

I believe the principles contained in this book will help you discover what destiny it is God has in store for your life. These principles are not just theory, they have been tested many times over in my own experience, and in the lives of those I live and work with. They are principles that can be put into practice right now.

I am a firm believer in divine guidance. The Bible teaches that God cares about the choices we make in life and that He has specific plans for us in every important choice we make. We can learn to hear God's voice, though it is not always easy. God's plans for us begin with His purposes for all mankind (Ephesians 1:11), and extend to the specific purposes He has for us as individuals (Isaiah 46:11; Psalm 40:5; Acts 16:6). Bible writers often speak of doing God's will, both in reference to obedience to God's precepts and principles, and also in relationship to specific obedience to something God wants us to do for Him (Psalm 40:8; Romans 12:1-2; 2 Corinthians 1:17; Romans 15:28, 29; Acts 13:2, 4; 2 Samuel 5:19).

God is committed to guiding us far more than we realize. He wants to teach us many lessons about His character and His ways. Psalm 32:8 says He is watching over us to ensure that we miss none of His blessing and plans for us. He wants us to do His will more than we do!

What is God's destiny for your life? Read on, and let's find out!

Chapter One

Ground Work for Guidance

Have you ever looked at a city skyline and marvelled at the buildings? Walls of reflective glass and massive concrete pillars looming ever upwards – colourful mosaics balanced against the sky. Seldom do we pause to wonder that for every towering office building there is a rigid frame of steel and cement holding it in place. The frame may be hidden from immediate view by all the glistening glass but, nevertheless, it is there, and if it were not the building would become a pile of shattered window panes and rubble.

So it is with guidance. Specific guidance is like the glass on a skyscraper – it is necessary but cannot support itself; it must have a structure beneath it. For the Christian, that support structure is made up of godly character and obedience to the revealed truth of God's Word. There are many things in life we don't need to pray about – we need to understand and obey. Most of God's will for our life is already revealed in the Bible.

Scripture reveals certain principles and truths that are God's will for us regardless of our personal situations and circumstances. Obedience to God in these areas, which I discuss in the following pages, is the prerequisite for knowing more of His will. To know God's will for the future, we must obey what we already know in the present!

As we look more closely at what God's Word says about His plan and purposes for our lives, let me suggest that you take a notebook and write the verse for each area at the top of a page. Prayerfully ask God to show you whether you are at present fulfilling His will in this area of your life. Refer back to your notebook on a regular basis and ask, 'Am I closer to God in this area now than I was six months ago?'

It is God's will that we believe in the Lord Jesus

'And this is His commandment, that we believe in the name of His Son Jesus Christ . . .' (1 John 3:23).

Belief in God and faith in His Son Jesus Christ is the most fundamental truth of the Bible, and without it we can never be Christians. Indeed, Christians in the early church were known as 'believers'. They heard of the things Jesus said and did, they read the letters the apostles and other eye witnesses wrote, and they *believed*.

The Philippian jailer asked, 'What must I do to be saved?' Paul's answer was refreshingly simple, 'Believe in the Lord Jesus and you shall be saved' (Acts 16:30–31). We must never forget that belief in the Lord Jesus is the cornerstone of our Christian faith and is therefore God's will for our lives. He wants a relationship with each one of us, and that is why He sent His Son into the world.

It is God's will that we give ourselves one hundred per cent to Him

'I urge you therefore, brethren, by the mercies of God, to present your bodies a living and holy sacrifice, acceptable to God, which is your spiritual service of worship' (Romans 12:1).

Many people want to know God's will to decide whether or not they will obey it! They have the attitude of 'Give me plenty of warning God. Tell me both sides of the story, and I'll decide and get in touch with you if I'm available.' God, however, expects unconditional surrender from us. The fact that Almighty God asks for our surrender should be enough to totally guarantee it! We are not two equals locked in debate; only pride can fool us into that delusion. We are finite, God is infinite. We are fallible, He is infallible. We waver, He is constant. We are the created, He is the creator. He is without fault and we are sinners, and He asks us to submit ourselves to His will because of who He is. He is the only wise God and He knows what is best for us in every situation of life.

God's purposes for mankind are always benevolent and merciful. He is for us, not against us (Romans 8:28–32). He longs to save and redeem people, and wants to see each of us reach our full potential. Because of His wonderful character, we can trust Him and have complete confidence in His character and His purpose for our lives.

God wants one hundred per cent of our life, not given out of fear, but out of love and gratitude for who

He is and what He has done on the cross. Christianity is not something we can ease into gradually. It is not a democracy where we give fifty-one per cent today, ten per cent next year, and so on until we have finally given ourself one hundred per cent to Him. If we dictate to God how much of our lives He can have then we have not surrendered at all. Instead, we have retained lordshp of our lives, and, even if we yield ninety-nine per cent of our lives to Him, we are still in control. Giving our lives 100% to the Lord does not mean we are perfect, it just means we are surrendered! What God wants to hear from us is, 'Anything, anytime, anywhere. I trust you Lord. You speak and I will obey.' Only when He hears can He fully guide our lives with specific directions.

It is God's will that we love the lost

'The Lord is not slow about His promise, as some count slowness, but is patient toward you, not wishing for any to perish, but for all to come to repentance' (2 Peter 3:9).

God yearns for people to hear the Gospel and be saved. What are we doing to see His will fulfilled in this area? Sharing the gospel is not the responsibility of a handful of 'professional' Christians, it is the responsibility of *all* Christians.

There are those Christians who have no difficulty sharing the gospel. They have an outgoing personality that enables them to preach on street corners, pray at their office desk, or pass out tracts to strangers in the subway. Many of us, however, are not that bold, yet we still have a responsibility to share His love with others.

God made each of us the way we are. He gave us our personality and we must find ways to share the gospel that are consistent with our personality. We may never stand and preach on a street corner, but we could pray for the person who does. We may be uncomfortable handing out tracts, but we culd volunteer to fold those tracts for the person who hands them out. In fact, we may never have anything to do with tracts and street meetings. God may want us to share the gospel with business associates. We could share a Christian record or magazine with a friend, or we could try to meet a specific need we know they have. There are hundreds of creative and effective ways to share the gospel and we must allow God to show us ways that are effective for us.

Youth With A Mission, the mission agency I work with has a strong emphasis on evangelism, but by no means are we all 'born evangelists'. However, each person in the mission is furthering the cause of the gospel. Some make dinner for drama teams, others write brochures to encourage people to participate in overseas outreaches. Still others prepare financial records and oversee day-to-day logistical operations. Our mission would be in total disarray if it were not for these people.

The same is true within the context of the local church. Not everyone can or wants to be, at the front preaching or leading a Sunday school class. Yet, everyone has their part to play. Perhaps there are children in the neighbourhood who would like to attend Sunday School if someone encouraged them and provided transport on Sunday mornings. The pastor cannot personally invite everyone in the area to attend church, but the combined effort of those in the church could mean an influx of potential converts. Each of us needs to pray and ask God for opportunities to do His will in the area of evangelism. Don't be deterred. You can, and must make a difference!

It is God's will that we do good works in Christ

'We are His workmanship, created in Christ Jesus for good works, which God prepared beforehand, that we should walk in them' (Ephesians 2:10).

James tells us faith without works is dead. Faith is the inward part of our Christian life, the part no one can see. Good works, on the other hand, are the outward part. Everyone can see our good works, or lack of them, but they cannot see the state of our faith.

Faith is like the roots of a tree, and works are the fruit. We don't judge how healthy a tree is by digging it up and inspecting its roots. Instead, we examine its fruit. If there is no fruit, we assume the roots to be diseased or dying. Likewise, if there are no good works visible in our lives as Christians, then our faith is in bad shape. If this is the case it is imperative we examine our faith and correct that problem lest our faith die altogether. Are we doing good works in the situation God has placed us in? They don't need to be spectacular, they can be simple things like babysitting a friend's children, or helping a neighbour get his car started on a cold morning. Seek out opportunities to serve others. Do good works in Jesus' name. If the prospect of doing good works doesn't excite you then you need to expose your roots of faith to the Holy Spirit and have Him tend them.

It is God's will that we grow spiritually

'Make every effort to supplement your faith with virtue, and virtue with knowledge, and knowledge with self-control, and self-control with steadfastness, and steadfastness with godliness, and godliness with brotherly affection, and brotherly affection with love' (2 Peter 1:5–7 RSV).

Some extremes in theological thinking suggest we ask the Lord into our lives and then sit back and wait for Him to take us to heaven. These verses certainly do not confirm that view. We are to make every effort to increase our faith, our knowledge, our self-control, our steadfastness, and our brotherly affection. Each of us is expected to take responsibility for our spiritual growth, be spiritually self-sustaining. We cannot rely on pastors or Christian leaders to keep our faith propped up. Some Christians live from Sunday to Sunday. They start their week ready for action, but by Saturday are drained of their enthusiasm and can barely drag themselves to church the next day for another boost. While this is not altogether unexpected in a new Christian, if it persists something is seriously amiss.

Paul talks of digesting the 'milk of the word', as compared to the 'meat of the world'. A baby needs someone to feed it milk, and in the same way, a new Christian needs someone to help them understand Biblical truth. We have all seen retarded adults who are incapable of feeding themselves. Behaviour that is natural and cute in an infant is pitiful and saddening to watch in these adults. Sadly, there are Christians who have not made 'every effort to supplement their faith', and they too are retarded in their spiritual development.

Prayer and Bible study are important in supplementing our faith. God reveals Himself to us in the Bible, and through prayer we have direct access to Him with our problems and questions. We must learn how to pray and intercede. There are many good books that can help us in establishing a personal prayer life. We need to read them and learn from them so that through prayer we can spiritually sustain ourselves.

Likewise, there are many good Bible Study guides that we can follow. Some go through the Bible book by book, others topic by topic. Try the different approaches and see which is the most rewarding for you, then stick with it. Once Bible study is a regular part of our lives we will begin to reap the rewards of a more stable and mature relationship with the Lord. We will also have the personal confidence to go to the Bible and find our own answers to life's questions.

God does not want us to be spiritually retarded and unable to sustain the new life He has given us. He wants us to reach a place of maturity where we can spiritually feed ourselves and be able to stand firm in the face of any adversity.

It is God's will that we submit to governing authorities

'Submit yourselves for the Lord's sake to every human institution, whether to a king as the one in authority, or to governors sent by him for the punishment of evildoers and the praise of those who do right. For such is the will of God that by doing right you may silence the ignorance of foolish men' (1 Peter 2:13–15).

I remember riding in a car along a Los Angeles freeway. I didn't know the driver very well, and before long he had the accelerator pedal down to the floor. As we sped along he glanced at me and explained apologetically that he had a 'demon of speed'. Not long afterwards a police car pulled in behind us. Miraculously, he brought his demon under instant control! 'It' was perfectly behaved until the police car turned off at an exit, then suddenly it flared up again! While this story has a funny side, it is also serious. We honour God by obeying those over us, even on the freeway.

As long as the governing authorities are honest and unselfish, most of us can submit to them; but what about submitting to the laws of men that contradict the laws of God? At that point we must put God's laws above the laws of men. Absolute obedience is only given to God. Governments are ordained by God for the good of mankind, and when they exploit and abuse their responsibilities and the people they govern, they must be held accountable both to God and to the people they serve.

Obedience to the laws of God may lead us to disobey the laws of men, or to be in conflict with what we are asked to do by the rulers over us. We must be prepared as Christians to resist unrighteousness, corruption, prejudice, immorality, oppression, and

17

every other form of evil. We should do that with love in our hearts, for the gospel is so radical that it commands us to love our enemies (Luke 6:32–36). That is what makes Christianity so powerful – we can submissively disobey, lovingly resist, passionately and intensely refuse to give in to evil men and corrupt systems, while we forgive those who are sinning against us.

It is God's will that we grow through trials and adversity

'Consider it pure joy, my brothers, whenever you face trials of many kinds, because you know that the testing of your faith develops perseverance. Perseverance must finish its work so that you may be mature and complete, not lacking anything' (James 1:2–4).

When faced with difficulties it is easy to question whether we really are in the will of God. But it is entirely possible to be in the will of God and still endure difficulties. Throughout our Christian life God will use difficult situations as a way of developing our characters, and we can never become mature Christians without them. There is no 'armchair correspondence course' for becoming a mature Christian – we must all go through struggles to get there. So, we must learn to embrace difficulties and trials as opportunities for developing spiritual muscle. We need these times and should not shy away from them. Don't pray for an easy life, pray for the strength to become a steadfast Christian.

'My son, do not regard lightly the discipline of the

Lord, nor faint when you are reproved by Him; For those whom the Lord loves He disciplines, and He encourages every son whom He receives' (Hebrews 12:5–6).

'So that no one would be unsettled by these trials. You know quite well that we were destined for them' (1 Thessalonians 3:3, NIV).

It is God's will that we follow His Spirit rather than our selfish desires

'So as to live the rest of the time in the flesh no longer for the lusts of men, but for the will of God' (1 Peter 4:2).

In life, we must choose to go in one of two directions. One direction has to do with the 'lusts of man', the other with doing 'the will of God'. The two are complete opposites. At one end of the scale we go our own way and enjoy what we consider to be the pleasures of life, and at the other end, we submit to the will of God and live our lives to please Him.

The word 'lust' is used today mainly in relation to sex, but its meaning is much broader than that. To lust is to passionately or overwhelmingly desire something. We can lust for a higher paying job, a new car, stereo, or any physical thing. We can even lust to 'get even' with another person. Living life in this way is living according to the lusts of the flesh.

Jesus tells us that unless we deny ourselves, take up the cross and live for Him, we are not fit for His kingdom. This may seem harsh and uncompromising, but, given this world's condition, is the only alternative we have. If we choose to ignore Jesus, and continue living to fulfil the lusts of the flesh, our lives will be marked by confusion, disappointment, heartache, and ultimately destruction.

Most non-Christians are accustomed to living freely by their feelings. If they desire something, they go after it. As Christians we are taught in the Bible to make our choices based on truth, not on what feels good. When a person first becomes a Christian there can be a tremendous inner conflict between these two ways of living. If we are accustomed to living by our feelings, we will not 'feel good' about the Christian life, but if we persist in putting truth above pleasure, after a time we will find our pleasure from truth!

It is God's will that we defend the rights of the poor

'Let us consider how to stimulate one another to love and good deeds, not forsaking our own assembling together, as is the habit of some, but encouraging one another; and all the more, as you see the day drawing near' (Hebrews 10:24–25).

It is God's will for us to do justice and to love mercy. 'He has shown you, O man, what is good. And what does the Lord require of you? To act justly and love mercy, to walk humbly with your God' (Micah 6:8).

We live in a world that is filled with injustice and inequality. As Christians, God calls us to make sure nothing we do contributes to the exploitation of those who are defenceless and poor (James 1:27, 5:1–6). In fact, we are commanded to defend the rights of the poor (Psalm 82:3). Because they are defenceless, we are to defend them (Proverbs 31:9). This will mean that at times there will, of necessity, be confrontation with those who oppress the poor. It is inevitable if we are defending those who are the victims of greed or oppression.

Because poverty creates hopelessness and lack of power over one's own life, a certain listlessness and apathy can result. It is dangerous to judge people quickly when they appear to be lazy. Perhaps they are suffering from the results of poor motivation, ignorance, despair, or bad parenting. Raising people out of such poverty requires great patience and mercy. That is one reason why the Lord commands us to 'love mercy'.

Further, 'doing justice' and 'loving mercy' does not mean we have all the answers. A paternalistic approach to the poor says as much about our needs as the needs of others. We have much to learn from all people. If we are to serve others we must not decide what their problems are and then impose our solutions. We are to serve all men from a basis of relationship. If we are not willing to take time to develop genuine friendships with the oppressed and poor in society, we should not try to get involved in their lives. We could do more harm than good.

It is God's will for us to love and forgive those who offend us

'That all of them may be one, Father, just as you are in me, and I am in you. May they also be in us so that the

21

world may believe that you have sent me. I have given them the glory that you gave me that they may be one as we are one. I in them and you in me. May they be brought to complete unity to let the world know that you sent me and have loved them even as you have loved me' (John 17:21–23).

'Be completely humble and gentle, be patient, bearing with one another in love' (Ephesians 4:2).

'Be kind and compassionate to one another, forgiving each other, just as in Christ, God forgave you' (Ephesians 4:3).

There is probably no area of life where it is more difficult to obey Biblical truth than in broken and difficult relationships. We are taught in the Bible to love our enemies and pray for those who persecute us (Luke 6:32–36, Matthew 5:46). If we are offended by someone, it is God's will for us to forgive them, and to keep on forgiving until we are healed of the hurt sustained in the relationship and we freely forgive them. We must choose to love the person we are offended by with God's love as an act of obedience and faith.

Some relationships come easy, and others have to be worked at. Love and unity do not happen by accident. It is a result of making the right choices over and over again. If we are involved in a destructive relationship, one that is damaging us emotionally or physically, God does not expect us to continue endlessly to expose ourselves to a harmful relationship. But even if we withdraw from a person because it is too painful, God still wants us to forgive them. By forgiving, we release bitterness from our lives and rise above the other person's faults and weaknesses (Proverbs 15:17–18, 14:7).

As we love and forgive one another, God's love is released into our lives and it becomes a powerful witness to the reality of His presence in our life. The preceding ten points are the will of God for each of us. Before God can use us or give us 'special assignments' He has to know if we can be trusted with what He has already given us. If we want to be used by God and enter into the destiny He has for our life, we must first take care of these basics.

Chapter Two

Three Ways to be Faithful

Recently a pastor relayed the following problem to one of our mission leaders: 'We have a young couple who came home from Youth With A Mission to raise financial support. They asked if the church would consider supporting them and in return they would commit themselves to the church for one year. We agreed to this arrangement. But, for the eight months they've been with us we only see them once a week – Sunday mornings. They don't offer to take Sunday school, go on the cleaning rota, or help with the youth group. If that's their idea of serving, then we feel used and don't think they have what it takes to be a missionary. We don't want to support them because they're not worth sending out as missionaries with your organization.'

When I heard of the situation I thought, 'The pastor is right. This couple does not deserve to be supported or to be full-time missionaries. They haven't been responsible. They haven't shown humility and proved themselves in the local church.'

We had to deal with the problem so one of our

leaders visited the couple. He pointed out to them the situation in which they had put the church missions board. He also visited the pastor who was very gracious and agreed to give the couple a second chance. The story had a happy ending. The couple stayed on at the church helping wherever they could and eventually were commissioned and sent out with the church's financial backing and blessing.

If we cannot serve God in the situation we're in right now, then what makes us think we can do better in a different location or position? Human tendency is to avoid the mundane and graduate to the spectacular, but that is not God's way. Godly character exemplified through the fruit of the Spirit can be as easily seen in small tasks as it can in large ones.

The best way to discover God's will for our lives is not by searching for it, but by serving where we are. Many of us have met people who claim they are called to do great things for God. However, while they're waiting for 'great things' to start happening they do nothing. They are unwilling to do anything 'less' than their 'calling'. But that is not God's way, He wants us to start out by being faithful in the small things.

Throughout the Bible, God promises positions and ministry to people, but seldom are the promises fulfilled immediately. There are often things in the character of the person that have to be worked out before they are ready to handle the ministry or position God has for them.

If we feel called to work with children then we should start where the need is. Arrive an hour before Sunday School and make sure the classrooms are clean

clean and the chairs are set out. Stack the chairs andsweep the floor afterwards. Be early for the Monday night prayer meeting, and any other relevant church activity during the week. By doing this we take the first steps towards knowing God's will – being an available servant.

Right now God wants to start training us for the future. He wants to develop in us the character strengths of stability, consistency and responsibility. These are traits most easily and efficiently developed in the local church. We do not become effective missionaries simply by crossing the sea: If we can't make it at home, we won't be able to make it somewhere else.

What areas of responsibility do we currently have? Are there relationships that need improving? Is there a missionary or church worker who needs encouragement? God wants to work in these areas of our life and prepare us for greater things. Take time and pray over the following three areas of faithfulness as preparation for doing more for the Lord.

One – faithful with little

If we are faithful in the little things God gives us to do now, He will give us more important ones in the future. In Matthew chapter 25 Jesus tells a parable about talents. A master gave each of his servants varying amounts of money before leaving on a long trip. They did not all receive the same amount of money, in much the same way as we all have differing levels of skill and ability. Upon his return the master inquired as to what his servants had done with the money he'd given them. He discovered that the first two servants had invested the money wisely and now had twice as much. The third, however, had buried his money and had only the amount the master had given him.

Jesus drew an interesting conclusion from this, 'For to everyone who has shall more be given, and he shall have an abundance; but from the one who does not have, even what he has shall be taken away' (Matthew 25:29).

Some have thought that if they only had a new car they'd look after it better than their present one. However, when a person gets a new car they find it doesn't take long before they treat it the same as they treated the old car. Why? Because they did not prove themselves with the old car. If they had disciplined themselves into taking care of the old car they would have no problem taking care of their new one. Similarly, many people believe in the principle of tithing, but do not personally tithe because they think they don't have enough money to start. But, the same principle applies – prove yourself with what you have and God will entrust you with more. If we wait until we have 'enough' money, we may never begin tithing. We must learn to be faithful with what God has already given us.

Two – faithful with things

'Whoever can be trusted with very little can also be trusted with much, and whoever is dishonest with little will also be dishonest with much. So, if you have not been trustworthy in handling worldly wealth, who will trust you with true riches?' (Luke 16:10–11).

Jesus tells us we must prove ourselves with physical things before we can be trusted with the true riches of spiritual gifts. If we prove faithful over mammon we can then be entrusted with spiritual responsibility. What is mammon? Mammon translated means 'riches', and more particularly, 'all the material things that riches can buy'.

Are we faithful over mammon? Some believe money to be an 'earthly thing' and not important to the Kingdom of God. In many ways, though, money is a Christian's apprenticeship to higher things. Therefore we must be good stewards of our material possessions. Do we pay our bills on time and are we scrupulously honest with our taxes? These life situations are God's test to see if we are ready for greater responsibility and trust in His kingdom. How we handle mammon does affect the way God can use us in His kingdom.

Three – faithful with other people's responsibilities

'And if you have not been trustworthy with someone else's property, who will give you property of your own?' (Luke 16:12).

It's easy to get spiritual when considering the will of God, but this verse puts things on a very practical level. Are we faithful with possessions that belong to other people? Do we borrow things and not return them? Are we more careless with others' possessions than we are with our own? Do we give our employer value for money, or are we lax on the job and leave early when he is not around? Do we follow instructions to the best of our ability, or are we always trying to do things our way? If we are not faithful in these areas, why do we suppose God will give us bigger tasks and more authority?

The most prominent pastors and spiritual leaders around the world today did not start out with high-profile ministries. They began by working under others and serving their vision. They proved themselves; they demonstrated they could be trusted to undertake and complete a task. As they did this, over time, they were recognized and given more authority. I believe this is the Biblical model – prove yourself capable of 'tending another man's vineyard', of serving the vision and calling of another, and God will give you your own.

The life of Joseph provides a picture of this principle at work. Through a dream, God gave Joseph a promise that his brothers would serve him. However, Joseph had much character development in store before he was ready for the fulfilment of that promise. Eventually he found himself in an Egyptian jail where, I'm sure, he spent a lot of time wondering what had gone wrong. During this time in jail God tested and prepared Joseph, and when he had proved himself faithful he was given a greater task with great authority. Notice, however, that Joseph ended up doing on a large scale exactly what he had proved himself faithful in doing while in jail – overseeing people and resources. Through his faithfulness he proved he was ready for the fulfilment of the promise, and his brothers did bow before him and serve him (Genesis 37–47).

King Saul also had promises made to him by God. We often cast Saul as the 'bad guy', forgetting he was given his position by God. The problem for Saul was that his character could not sustain the authority God entrusted to him. Despite repeated opportunities to prove himself he failed and God was eventually forced to remove the power, authority and blessing he had bestowed upon Saul.

Many think that once they get a position they'll rise to the occasion, and do and be everything God requires of them. The story of Saul, however, illustrates that this is not true. Position and authority may only compound areas of weakness in our character, and we would be better off dealing with them before we pursue any ministry. To do so will save much heartache and embarrassment.

Unlike Saul, David knew God had called him to be king, but did not seek the kingship. Instead, he trusted God to bring it about. On several occasions David had an opportunity to kill Saul and claim the position God had promised, but he did not. He wanted to receive it in God's way and in God's time and eventually his patience and faithfulness were rewarded.

God's promises to us are never an excuse to ride over others in pursuit of them. God will fulfil his word to us in due time. Testing and proving come first, and we dare not attempt to short cut them. God wants to hear each of us say, 'I'll do this your way.

It's your promise, and I trust you to bring it about.'

What happens if we know God has called us to be a missionary but our spouse is not interested, or we have obligations to family; what do we do? Do we give up on what God has promised? If God has called us then He will use us regardless of the circumstances. He wants us to be faithful even if what we can do seems so little in comparison to the things we could do were our circumstances more favourable. Perhaps there's a nearby community of the same ethnic group God has called us to. We could attend church there and get involved in outreach and visitation, or we could enrol in a language school and learn their language. When God sees us being faithful He can move to rectify those circumstances that have hampered our going overseas, and when we finally get there we will be so much better prepared.

Ten years ago Mark felt God call him to minister in China. At that time it was very difficult for a Westerner to go to China as a tourist, let alone as a missionary. Nevertheless, Mark trusted God and began looking for practical ways in which he could prepare himself. He went to the library, borrowed Mandarin language tapes and began learning the language. He read all the books the library had on life in China.

About five or six years ago the doors to China began to open, and Mark was there, equipped and ready. He applied to the Chinese government for a job teaching English as a second language, for which he was accepted and sent to a remote province. Mark is still in China today. He has free access to the student dormitories where he holds evening Bible studies. As a result of his efforts he has been able to lead many of his student friends to a relationship with Jesus Christ. Had Mark been unfaithful and failed to take the initiative when God spoke to him he would not be doing what he is doing in China today.

Faithfulness is like the hinge on a door. It is only a small thing yet without it even the largest of doors will not open. By being faithful in all God has presently spoken to us we make a hinge on which He can swing the door wide open for us in the future. Faithfulness is a highly prized virtue in God's kingdom.

Chapter Three

On Special Assignment

There is a segment of the Body of Christ which has what I call 'the martyr complex'. These Christians automatically know God is going to force them to do the very thing they hate most. If they like warm weather, God will obviously call them to Alaska, or, if they like working with gadgets and machines, they're destined to spend the rest of their life on a remote Pacific island where there are no electric sockets.

We must be very careful with this kind of attitude lest we misrepresent God's character and portray Him as a gigantic 'killjoy'. There may be times when God requires us to do something we do not enjoy and would not naturally choose, but since God created us to be the kind of people we are, as a general rule He pays careful attention to our personalities and natural gifts when He gives us special assignments.

What are our gifts and abilities? And what special assignment does God have for us? Many find it hard to answer these questions because it is difficult to get a balanced and objective view of ourselves. Sometimes we think we're better at something than we really are, or conversely, we fail to recognize our strengths and abilities.

The following points will help us in recognizing what our strengths and weaknesses, gifts and abilities are. They will also give us a clearer picture of where God may want to use us.

Have an honest estimation of yourself

We all know people who have unrealistic estimations of their abilities and gifts. We've heard of the choir member with the worst voice singing with the most gusto, the person who has no rapport with children volunteering to run the Sunday School, much to the chagrin of the children. Why, we wonder, can't they see their lack of talent for the job?

When evaluating themselves, people tend to swing towards one of two extremes. They either underestimate or overestimate their abilities, and both are debilitating. We are admonished in scripture not to think more highly of ourselves than we ought. Yet, today there are many Christians sitting in pews doing nothing because they feel they haven't been offered a position that is worthy of them. They have an overestimation of their abilities. In waiting to be recognized, they are in grave danger of missing God's opportunity for them.

Conversely, we should not think more lowly of ourselves than we ought. Many people are waiting in the wings until they feel more worthy, or they have more talents to offer. However, talents and abilities are both discovered and developed by stepping out and doing something that needs to be done. It is not a sign of spirituality to deny to ourselves or others the gifts God has given us. If we're the best person, then we should not be coy about it. Instead, we should give the job our best. Perhaps others somewhere could do a better job, but God prizes our availability. Through launching out we learn new things about ourselves and gain a fuller understanding of our talents and abilities.

Listen to what others say about you

The people God places around us are like a mirror. They reflect back to us, through their comments and insights, what our natural gifts and strengths are. While we should never be governed solely by another person's opinion of us, those opinions can, nonetheless, prove valuable in assessing our strengths and weaknesses. Listen to what other people have to say about us, both the positive and negative. What do we receive the most compliments for? Keep a record and begin to see what talents others see in you.

Are you a good listener? Do people come to you with their problems? Have you ever considered enrolling in a counselling class? As we learn more about our areas of strength and weakness ask God where it is those strengths could be best used.

When people point out areas of weakness to us we shouldn't dismiss it as malicious slander. There is often much truth in their observations, even if their intent for sharing is dubious. Talk to the Lord about the things people say to us, especially if the same comment comes from more than one person. Take the initiative and discuss your weaknesses with others. Maybe we're not suited for what we are currently doing, and perhaps God wants to shift us into a job or ministry that will bring more fulfilment and fruit in our lives but He is waiting for us to humble ourselves and admit our weaknesses.

The observations and insights of those around us are important if we are to have a balanced and accurate assessment of ourselves. To receive the full value of their input we must first listen to them, and then ask God for His input on the matter.

Be the person God intended you to be

It is good to be inspired by others, but that is not to say we should try and imitate them. God created each of us uniquely different from everyone else and we insult Him when we spend years trying to imitate others or contort ourself into being something He never intended us to be. We each have many and varied gifts, and we will never discover exactly what they are if we're always copying others. The great moves of God in the past have been spearheaded by men and women who dared to be themselves.

During the last century Hudson Taylor pioneered a new era in missions. His ideas were radical and unacceptable to the great majority of his peers. Undeterred by this, he persisted and founded the China Inland Mission which became the forerunner of today's missionary societies. Had Taylor been more concerned about the way others perceived him he would never have left the shores of England. Instead, freed from self-doubt and the worry that no one else had ever done what he was about to do, he became all that God intended him to be – the father of much of our modern missionary endeavour.

The same is true of William Booth, founder of the Salvation Army. His challenge to the social ills of nineteenth-century England changed the course of a nation. Despite his success, Booth and the methods he employed, were scorned by the Christians of his day. They felt he was too extreme, and much too opinionated. But, where would England be today if there had not been men for the Salvation Army?

Being all that God intended us to be in not always easy, but the rewards are always great.

Take seriously your natural gifts and desires

Sometimes when people come to me for advice on guidance I tell them, 'Take seriously your natural desires. What do you enjoy doing? Do what you like!' They're often stunned by this, but they shouldn't be. God created each of us and if we have a desire to do something, and the abilities to carry it out, then He could well want us to do it for His glory. God does not give us talents and abilities only to taunt us.

In trying to discover what it is God wants us to do in life we sometimes overlook the obvious. This is particularly true of people who become Christians later in life. They associate all they've done in the past with their sinful lifestyle, and, in their desire to leave it all behind, sometimes fail to see that God has given them gifts to use for His Kingdom. Because we have used our gifts outside the Kingdom of God this does not mean they're of no further use. Indeed, the opposite is true. However, our gifts first need to be sanctified and made available for use in the service of others.

Steve was a young man who had been heavily involved in rock music. He was an excellent guitarist, but after becoming a Christian gave away his guitar and vowed never to play it again. After several years of discipling he began to feel a yearning to buy another guitar and start playing again. He was cautious about this since he associated the guitar with his former lifestyle. As he prayed, God showed him several things. Firstly, every good gift comes from God, and He wanted Steve to use the gifts He had given him. Secondly, Steve's musical talents had been given to him for a purpose, and through failing to acknowledge and use them he was not being all God had created him to be. Steve saw that he had been blessed with musical talent and simply because he had used it for the devil did not mean God no longer had a use for it. However, his time away from music had allowed him to establish his identity in Christ.

Steve did go back to his musical career, and with strong Christian support, has been an effective witness for Christ. His natural gift, coupled with God's anointing are a powerful combination.

God has a special assignment for each of us and as we understand the gifts, strengths and abilities God has given each of us we are in a better position to see areas where we are suited for service in His Kingdom.

Assess the desires of your heart to see if they are godly. Share them with those around you, and seek wise counsel. Above all, keep praying. If they are God-given desires, begin to use your gifts for the Lord. Don't try and force ahead, but seek opportunities to serve in the areas in which God has gifted you.

As we serve others, as we make ourselves available to help where needed most, as we offer the skills and gifts God has given us to serve in His Kingdom as light in the world, we will be led by God into His will. He will lead us! That is His promise!

Chapter Four

Specific Guidance

We all want to know the answer to the question, 'Lord, what do you want me do?' Some will open the book to this chapter first, impatient to find personal guidance, and assuming the previous chapters irrelevant in the search. Yet, as those who have read the book thus far know, the earlier chapters form the basis upon which we can have confidence to step out in the area of divine guidance. Before we can construct any superstructure, the foundations must be firmly laid. There are times when we can do without the superstructure, but we can never do without the foundation of righteous living.

Imagine a young man taking a driving test. His instructor gives him one last piece of advice before he takes the test, 'Tom, obey all road signs.' Tom gets into the car with the examiner and waits. After a time the examiner asks him is he knows how to start the car. Tom assures him he does, and continues to wait. The examiner, becoming impatient, responds, 'If this is some kind of game I'm not amused. Either get the car started, or get out.' Tom is shocked and tells the examiner that his driving instructor told him to obey all signs, so, he is waiting for a sign to tell him to start the car.

Ridiculous you say, nobody could be that stupid. Yet, many of us are like that at times. We want to hear a voice booming from heaven telling us what to do next. Had Tom started the car and driven off he would have found road signs with instructions to obey, and even if he found no signs, that's no excuse for him to stop driving, since there are unposted road rules that must be obeyed for the safety of all. Similarly in life, there are times when we experience direct indisputable guidance, and other times when we must simply follow the rules for living the Christian life. By both means we reach our destination.

Hearing the right voice

The Bible teaches that there are three different sources or 'voices' we can hear – the voice of God, the voice of Satan, and the voice of fleshly desires (or human desires that are good, but may not be God's best for us). The task for us is to recognize and know which voice is which.

A voice that constantly tells us to avoid anything that places a demand on our lives, and urges us to take the easy way out of things is most likely the voice of the flesh. This voice encourages us to pamper ourselves and listen to the promises of God without taking note of the conditions associated with them. God has promised to give us the desires of our heart –

yes – but when our hearts are wholly His, our desires are also in harmony with His.

When I am seeking God's direction, I like to express to God in prayer my need and dependence upon Him to guide me. I express my faith in Him to guide me and I consciously choose to die to any selfish desires or presumption that would keep me from knowing His will. I also pray against Satan and ask God to protect me from his wiles. I exercise the authority we are given as believers to bind Satan and resist his influence and his evil ways (James 4:7, 1 Peter 5:8–9, Ephesians 6:10–20).

Though we should not approach major decisions with fear or unbelief in our hearts, we should be very careful to seek God in prayer. Prayer is God's way for us to commune with Him. He desires that we seek Him, sharing our thoughts and desires with Him. Since prayer is conversing with God, we should give God a chance to speak to us as well. There should be times of stillness and quiet, listening to God through meditation, Bible study, and prayerful expectant silence. Do we pray without expecting God to speak to us? Do we believe He can speak to us? If so, should we not wait for him to speak?

We should never make a decision based on one impression in a time of prayer. We should test those impressions through seeking the counsel of godly people, reading God's word, having peace from the Lord in our hearts, and the use of our minds to analyse what God is leading us to do.

There have been times when my desires have not been in line with God's desires. In 1975, when I felt

God wanted me to leave Amsterdam and move to the countryside I did not want to go. I had been brought up in Long Beach, California, and was a city boy through and through. To me the city was where the action was and I loved Amsterdam. The countryside was a nice place to visit for a week, but I had no desire to live there! I struggled inside and part of me said; 'This is the will of God, He is leading me to the countryside,' and yet another part said; 'I'm doing something effective here. What good will sitting on a farm do me or anyone else?' In the end I was honest with the Lord about my doubts and fears and lack of desire, and in that time of honesty I began to see things from God's perspective, which in turn, changed the way I felt about the move He wanted me to make. A peace began to grow in my heart and I began to see how the decision was consistent with goals and objective we had set for our work.

Our attitude when seeking guidance is also crucial. If we come to God in faith and humility He promises to speak to us. But if we come with presumption in our hearts, we are more likely to hear the voice of Satan, the author of presumption. The Bible teaches that Satan is an angel of light. He won't just tempt us with blatant sin but also with subtle deception.

God seldom hurries us when He speaks and gives direction. Normally He allows us ample time to weigh the decision that must be made, and come to a place of confidence about what He's asked us to do. Conversely, Satan urges us to rush ahead with things without fully weighing and considering them. God guides, while Satan, and sometimes others as well, drives. So, if we feel an unnatural urgency about something to the extent that we don't even want to take the time and seek counsel or pray further about it, then we should be suspicious about whose voice we are really hearing. One thing Satan does not want us to do is to pray about things. 'It is a snare for a man to say rashly, "It is holy!" and after the vow to make inquiry' (Proverbs 20:25).

One of Satan's favourite tactics is confusion. If we're not sure about something, the best thing to do is wait. If it is the right thing to do, God will confirm it. Likewise, if after making a decision we believe to be in the will of God, we feel depressed and confused we should wait and ask God to confirm the decision to us.

God's voice has a liberating effect. Even when He asks us to do something difficult there is a sense of confidence and expectancy about what lies ahead. We may not think it wise to share what He is asking us to do with everyone, but we should at least be able to share it with those we respect as mature Christians. If we cannot share our guidance with anyone else, beware, something is wrong.

Let's look at some of the ways God speaks to his people.

God speaks in the quietness of the heart and mind
Most often, God speaks in the quietness of the heart to those He has the confidence will do what He asks. However, we should not put God into a box. He is free to guide us whenever, wherever, and however He chooses. And when He speaks He will not obscure things from us so that we have to puzzle over them for

weeks trying to understand what it is He has said. When God speaks He is clear and specific. Do not get trapped into the practice of analysing every event and circumstance that happens in life to see if God is speaking. From time to time God will use circumstances as a way of guiding us; however, we will know when those times are and will not have to go looking for them. God speaks through our own minds. He will plant thoughts and ideas in our minds as we prayerfully seek Him. It is often wise to analyse a decision carefully considering the pros and cons. This is a time to apply Biblical principles to the decisions we are making, and to use some sanctified common sense.

As we prepare to make an important decision it is wise to list all the factors involved, such things as: who would be affected, how long would it take, what changes would take place, why should there be a change, and what would be accomplished? After you make the list, go through and prioritize the factors. What is the most important to you and why?

Some very important 'principle' type questions to apply to this process are as follows:

Will it honour God?
Will it help people?
Have I listened to wise counsel?
Have I included close friends?
What are my motives?
Can it be done with integrity?
Is it worth doing?
Can I do it in unity with those I fellowship with?

Do I have the gifts and abilities?

Is it the right time?

Is this decision consistent with the objectives I
   have prayerfully set for my life?

Would it undermine other commitments?

Fleeces

The Book of Judges chapter 6 tells the story of how
Gideon placed a fleece on the ground overnight and
asked God to saturate it with dew while the surrounding ground remained dry. The next night he asked God
to reverse the process, leaving the fleece dry while the
surrounding ground was wet with dew. Why did
Gideon do this? Because his life depended upon
knowing what it was God wanted him to do and at
what time. Gideon was about to lead Israel into a
potentially devastating battle against the Midianites.
Reading through the chapter we find that Gideon used
the fleece as a means of confirming what he already
believed to be the will of God for the situation.

If we are to use 'fleeces' in our guidance then this is
the proper Biblical context for their use. They are a
means of confirming what already seems apparent to
us as the will of God in a situation. By no means are
they to be used as a way of getting fresh guidance
from God. They are not the lazy way or short cut to
finding God's will. Seeking the Lord in this manner
can be an indication of a lack of faith or a lack of
teaching. God wants us to grow in maturity and
wisdom so that the decisions we make in life can be
directed by Biblical principles or hearing God's voice
directly to our mind and heart.

I heard of a young man who had to drive through a set of street lights on his way to college. Each morning he would pray, 'God if you want me at school today make the light green. If it's red I'll assume you want me to play squash instead.' That is not a Biblical 'fleece'!

Financial provision

Financial provision is another way God can confirm his will to us. If we are planning a new venture but do not have the necessary funds to cover it, provision of those funds can confirm it as God's direction. However, finances should be confirmation, not guidance itself. We should not look to money to guide, but the Lord.

I remember my first foreign outreach with Youth with a Mission which was to Jamaica. I discussed the prospect of going with my father, and while he was right behind my desire to go he made it clear that it was not going to by '*my*' faith and '*his*' finances that got me there! Later as I grew in my faith I saw how wise his counsel was.

After talking with my father a phrase I'd heard came to mind, 'If you do the possible God will do the impossible.' As a result I set about raising as much money as I could. My friends and I collected junk and we had a garage sale. I took my old basketball trophies and tried to sell them – I quickly found out nobody wants secondhand trophies! As I did this God began to release the finance I needed. One lady gave me a shoe box that contained several hundred dollars in coins – tips she'd collected as a waitress.

The most humbling experience, though, was when

47

R. T. Cummings, a friend in my Church, signed his monthly injury compensation cheque over to me. It was all his family had to live on for the next month and at first I refused to take it. R.T. insisted, saying if I had the faith to go, then he had the faith to stay. 'I can trust God just like you can,' he declared.

As I boarded the bus in Los Angeles I had enough money to get me as far as Miami. I would travel there and if the Lord provided the rest of my fare along the way I would fly on to Jamaica. From a bus depot in Texas I called my father who told me excitedly of a non-Christian relative who had just visited him. He had told the relative about my trip but made no mention of my financial needs. He had assumed the relative would not be interested in helping me financially, but to his surprise the relative had offered to write a cheque for me. Neither of them knew how much I needed so I was both surprised and excited when I found out that my relative's cheque covered my remaining travel costs and outreach fees to the last penny. I travelled on to Jamaica with a sense of awe in my heart; I knew I was in the centre of God's will – He had worked on my behalf.

I learned that my need was met through fellowship as well as through faith. Not only had God moved on my behalf, but R. T. Cummings who had given so sacrificially to me also saw God provide food, funds, and clothing. The Cummings family had not lacked for one thing during the whole month I was gone. There have been many more financial tests along the way, but as a teenager on my first overseas outreach I learned first hand that God will provide if we just step out in faith. I did not step out presumptuously. I knew God wanted me to attend that outreach and I did my part as well, so His provision was indeed a confirmation to me of His will.

Scriptures

God can use specific passages of His Word to speak to us. They can speak to our situation through our daily readings or God can impress specific passages on our minds as we wait on Him in prayer. It is important not to make the mistake of interpreting the meaning of the passage by how it is used to speak to us in a specific situation. God is gracious to speak to us from passages out of context, but that does not constitute a principle of interpretation.

Peace

God will always give peace to our hearts when we are doing His will. His presence brings peace and when we have prayed and thought through a decision, we can expect God to confirm the right choice with a peace that gives us confidence even in the midst of difficulty.

Dreams and visions

God can also use dreams and visions as a means of speaking to us. Again in this realm it is important that the dream or vision be confirmation of what we already believe to be the will of God for us, or, if it seems to be fresh guidance, that we seek other confirmation of the guidance from God. The realm of dreams and visions is very subjective and if we do not take these precautions Satan can easily confuse us.

Jeff was a young man who felt God had called him to a specific ministry within Youth With A Mission. He wrote to the ministry explaining how he felt called and asking for an application form. Several weeks went by and there was no reply. Then one night Jeff had a dream. In the dream he received a letter from the ministry which he opened. Inside was an application form and a covering letter which told him that while they had enclosed an application form there was no chance of his being able to join the ministry in the foreseeable future. During the dream Jeff also heard a voice telling him he would receive a letter from the ministry the next day, that it would read as it had in the dream, and that he was not to heed it. Instead, he was to fill out the application form and take it to the ministry in person.

The next morning Jeff was waiting for the mail to arrive and sure enough there was his letter from the ministry. He anxiously tore it open and inside was a letter that read almost exactly as he had seen in his dream. It said there was an accommodation shortage and as a result they were unable to take on any new staff. Jeff's friends found his elation at being turned down hard to understand! They did not realize the letter was God's confirmation to him that he would be part of the ministry. He filled out the application and did as the Lord had instructed him to do with it. Jeff was accepted on to the staff of the ministry within three weeks and still serves with Youth With A Mission today. The dream confirmed to Jeff that his guidance was right and gave him the encouragement he needed to pursue it.

Some Cautions Regarding Guidance

1. Don't plan your life around a blueprint. Seek security and direction in a person, not a detailed plan or programme. We need a guide, not a road map, and Jesus is that guide.
2. Obey the truth we know, as a basis for knowing God's will for the future.
3. There are times when it is not clear what to do next in life. Sometimes God will test us to see if we trust Him and will walk in faith.
4. Don't make demands or set deadlines with God.
5. When going through a rough time, don't doubt what God has directed you to do previously. In other words, when in a time of spiritual darkness, don't turn away from what God has shown you in the light.
6. Don't be proud. Don't say, 'If this is not God's will, I have never heard His voice.' We can all make mistakes. Be prepared to admit you are wrong. That is our greatest protection!
7. Don't use the wrong means for the right end. Cheating in exams to get a degree to serve God is not God's will.
8. Don't confuse hormones with holiness. How often have we heard the words, 'God told me I was to marry him,' and it was not God's will?
9. Don't confuse the 'movement' with the 'moment'. Seek God's timing as well as the right thing to do.
10. Don't get too super-spiritual. Learn to be practical as well as being open to hearing God's

voice. If *He* speaks to you, *He* will confirm His voice through *other godly people*.

11. Don't act independently. Be a person who is accountable to others.

12. Don't get caught up in spiritual verbosity. Be practical and wise in the way you communicate your desire to do God's will. Using common sense expressions and terms to express our sense of guidance helps keep us balanced. Besides, declaring God has told us to do something can not only be proud, it can also cut off a process of discussion and counsel with other Christians. It is hard to disagree or counsel a person who declares unequivocally that God has told them to do something. It isolates us from much needed counsel and input from others.

Unfulfilled Promises

What should we do when we feel we have had a definite promise from God that has not yet come to pass?

There are many instances in scripture where a considerable amount of time lapsed between the promise of something and its fulfilment. In fact, the rule seems to be: promise plus preparation equals fulfilment. After God has given us a promise He sets about preparing us to receive it. If we study the lives of any of the great Bible characters we see this truth illustrated over and over again. Consider the lapse of time between God telling Noah about the flood and the actual occurrence of that flood. Yet, it was knowledge of the flood, and the promise that his family would be spared that propelled Noah to build the ark. The promise was given, Noah completed the required work, and the promise was fulfilled.

Jesus told Peter he would be a 'Rock'. However, Peter had much preparation to go through before that promise was fulfilled. Likewise, the rest of the disciples had three and a half years of preparation before they were ready for all God had promised them. When we have a promise from God we should hold on to it, co-operate in any needed preparation, and allow the Lord to bring the fulfilment of the promise.

Another aspect of timing and the will of God is waiting for God's opportunity. In college I played basketball, and one of the teams we played against was from the University of Florida. One of the players on the Florida team was under consideration to be an All-American Basketball player and our team was eager to meet him. We had expected a very tall and muscular player, but to our surprise he wasn't. Indeed, from first appearances there seemed to be little that was remarkable about this player and we were all a little disappointed. As the game commenced I noticed that he wasn't even fast on his feet. But he possessed an uncanny ability to be in the right place at the right time. If a team was moving one way and the ball bouncing another, he was right there where the ball was. His hands were up to catch the ball when they should be, and if it came bouncing to the floor he was there to pick it up, and that is what made him a great player.

God wants us to be like that basketball player. He wants us to have the spiritual alertness that puts us in the right place at the right time when the Spirit is wanting to do something. As we seek His direction we need to distinguish between the right thing to do, and the right time to do it. God may put a plan or desire in our hearts, but we should not presume that means we do it immediately. God may be preparing our hearts and we are to take plenty of time to think, discuss, and ponder what is stirring in our hearts.

Chapter Five

Leadership, Guidance and the Sovereignty of God

An internationally recognized Bible teacher ministered among a group I was working with. I can still recall her, as she was praying with the group of people, going over to one young couple and giving them some very specific counsel she felt God had laid on her heart for them. The young couple were somewhat confused by what she said so after the service they went and talked further with the woman. 'What you said to us doesn't make any sense.' I watched for her reaction and very graciously, with no hint of self-defence, she replied, 'I felt strongly that I needed to share that with you, but I could be wrong. I've been wrong before. Submit it to the Lord. If it is from Him, He will confirm it in other ways. If it is not, then I apologize.'

As I listened I thought, 'Here's a woman with a reputation who isn't afraid of being wrong. She's not pushing her ministry as the infallible word of God.' My admiration for, and confidence in her ministry grew greatly. We can all be wrong at times, but it takes a person who fears God more than their reputation to admit to it.

Any leader, regardless of how well known and trusted they are, cannot make all our decisions for us. We are responsible before God for our own guidance, and it is both dangerous and foolish to take that responsibility lightly, or abdicate it altogether and let another do it for us.

God may, at times, use a leader to give us guidance or confirm something He has been saying to us. A leader who claims to hear the voice of God for others and then encourages them to act quickly on it, should sound loud warning bells for every Christian. We must never allow another to violate our sense of caution and intuition and bully us into doing something we're unsure of. God watches over us, and we must never allow anyone to take His place. The results of doing so can be disastrous.

The tragedy of people slavishly in bondage to cults bears witness to this. They have unreservedly handed their personal freedom and responsibility over to someone who claims to have cornered the market on spiritual truth. As time goes by they lose their ability to think clearly and make decisions for themselves. They are psychological cripples addicted to the pseudo-spiritual platitudes their human 'god' feeds them. That is not what God intended. He created our minds and he expects us to use them. Indeed it is He who says, 'Come now, and let us reason together' (Isaiah 1:18). He wants us to serve Him not out of some slavish bondage whereby we surrender to Him even our ability to think; He wants us to serve Him because we have reasoned together and have come to see and understand that He is right and as such is worthy of our allegiance.

Hearing God's voice in specific guidance does not necessarily signify spirituality, or God's stamp of approval. On the contrary, a study of the Bible reveals that spectacular guidance is often reserved for the hard-headed and rebellious.

Consider Balaam and his ass. The ass was quicker than Balaam to receive the angel's message. When the angel finally got Balaam's attention he told him he would sooner have killed him than talk to him! With that introduction the angel went on to give specific instructions to Balaam about what to say when he reached Balak. Obviously it was not Balaam's spirituality that singled him out for God's special direction, it was his rebellion!

Likewise Saul, on the road to Damascus, received a vision and was temporarily blinded. We think, 'Oh, Paul. He was a great man of God.' But he was not at that stage. He was a ruthless hater of Christians who was present when Stephen was stoned to death. God did not single him out because he was righteous, but because of the unrighteousness He wanted to change.

There are also many recorded instances where God gives spiritually mature men and women guidance to carry out specific tasks. The Book of Acts has many inspiring examples of guidance: Paul's call to Macedonia; Peter's vision of the unclean foods, and subsequent visit to Cornelius' house.

Sometimes guidance is given as a stamp of approval, and other times as a mark of discipline. We must always remember that we cannot force God's hand as to how He will deliver guidance, and we must be wary of making heroes of those God guides in more spectacular ways than others.

The bottom line in guidance

'My shield is with God, who saves the upright in heart' (Psalm 7:10).

There are pitfalls in the area of guidance. For every method of guidance, we can name someone who has tried it and failed. But therein lies the problem. Guidance is not some kind of horoscope or divining rod we pull out every time we want to know something about the future. Guidance is purely and simply God communicating to us about very specific matters. Most of God's will for our lives is already revealed in the Bible. The point of this book is not to furnish us with methods of guidance, its point is to illuminate ways God can speak to us and to help us recognize when He does. The only effective 'method' of guidance I know is living our lives wholeheartedly for God. If we do this then assuredly we will know His guidance in our life. If we seek God sincerely, God will get through to us. He wants us to grow, but He also wants to help us find His will for our lives! The most important thing to God is our openness to obey Him, and a teachable spirit.

Each of us needs God's direction in life, and should He choose to lead us by way of a different route than we are presently on we must be willing to follow. It is easier to change the direction of something already in motion than something that is stationary. As every parent can attest it's easier to get the child cleaning the car to stop and run an errand than it is to get the child who is lazy to do it. Likewise, if we are striving to hear God's voice, and, at the same time, doing our best to please Him, then we are more likely to hear His voice and respond to it.

'Trust in the Lord with all your heart, and do not lean on your own understanding. In all your ways acknowledge Him, and He will make your paths straight' (Proverbs 3:5–6).

Chapter Six

Where To From Here?

We have seen that there is a place for both general and specific guidance in the Christian life, and that one should not be emphasized at the expense of the other. I like to think of guidance and the Christian life this way.

Imagine I receive an invitation to visit my friend who lives at 270 Imperial Road, Madras, India. I decide to accept the invitation. The first thing I do is not to go and buy a map of Madras to locate Imperial Road, it is to make reservations on a flight to India. Once I get to India I make my way to Madras, and once in Madras I locate Imperial Road. After arriving at Imperial Road I find number 270 where my friend lives.

Our Christian life is a journey and we can make the mistake of focusing so closely on the specifics of the journey that we fail to see the broad picture. The specifics are there, just as 270 Imperial Road is in Madras, India. However, unless I get to Madras, any street map with the specific location of Imperial Road on it is of little use to me. All of us would like to know where we will be and what we'll be doing in ten years' time, but we must live in the reality of where we are today. Our security is to be in a person, not a plan. Begin to move in the direction you feel God is leading you, and as you move along listen and ask God for more specific directions.

A trip begins with the first step, regardless of whether or not we know the location of our final destination. The important thing in getting to any destination is beginning, and keeping our eyes on the one who's guiding us – the Lord Jesus.

We may not always be certain of our final destination, but we are always certain of how God wants us to conduct ourselves on the journey and we can be absolutely and totally confident of His love for us and His commitment to guide and direct our lives. Our ultimate victory is assured – as long as we keep our hearts open to the Lord Jesus. We are sons and daughters of the living God and He has made it very plain in scripture how we are to live. Refer often to the ten points in Chapter One which form a checklist we can use throughout our Christian life to keep us heading in the right direction. God has a plan for our lives, and once we are moving He can lead us into it.

'"For I know the plans that I have for you," declared the Lord, "plans for welfare and not for calamity to give you a future and a hope"' (Jeremiah 29:11).

RICH IN FAITH

Colin Whittaker

Colin Whittaker's persuasive new book is written for ordinary people all of whom have access to faith, a source of pure gold even when miracles and healing seem to happen to other people only.

The author identifies ten specific ways to keep going on the road to faith-riches, starting where faith must always begin—with God himself, the Holy Spirit, the Bible, signs and wonders, evangelism, tongues and finally to eternal life with Christ.

OUR GOD IS GOOD

Yonggi Cho

This new book from Pastor Cho describes the blessings, spiritual and material, that reward the believer. Yonggi Cho presents his understanding of the fullness of salvation, bringing wholeness to God's people.

HEARTS AFLAME
Stories from the Church of Chile

Barbara Bazley

Hearts Aflame is a book suffused with love for the large, sometimes violent country of Chile and joy at the power of the Gospel taking root.

Each chapter is a story in itself, telling of some encounter, episode of friendship that has left its mark on the author's life.

If you wish to receive *regular information* about *new books*,
please send your name and address to:

London Bible Warehouse
PO Box 123
Basingstoke
Hants RG23 7NL

Name..

Address ....

....

....

....

I am especially interested in:
- ☐ Biographies
- ☐ Fiction
- ☐ Christian living
- ☐ Issue related books
- ☐ Academic books
- ☐ Bible study aids
- ☐ Children's books
- ☐ Music
- ☐ Other subjects